Ten Unusual Features of LuLu McDunn

Dog Legs Ink An Imprint of Gauthier Publications
Saint Clair Shores, MI

Gauthier Publications
P.O. Box 806241
Saint Clair Shores, MI 48080
Attention: Permissions Department

Frog Legs Ink is an imprint of Gauthier Publications
www.FrogLegsInk.com

Proudly printed and bound in the USA

ISBN: 978-0-9820812-7-3
Printed in Brainerd, MN (July 2010)

Library of Congress Cataloging-in-Publication Data

Pulley, Kelly.
 Ten unusual features of Lulu McDunn / by Kelly Pulley. -- 1st ed.
     p. cm.
 Summary: Rhyming text counts the odd characteristics of Miss Lulu McDunn's face and body, in each of which she finds something good.
 ISBN 978-0-9820812-7-3 (hardcover : alk. paper)
 [1. Stories in rhyme. 2. Self-esteem--Fiction. 3. Individuality--Fiction. 4. Counting.] I. Title.
 PZ8.3.P956Ten 2010
 [E]--dc22
                    2010028792

For Whitney, Amanda,
Kate and Sean.

Miss Lulu McDunn had a very odd face
and a few of her parts seemed a bit out of place.
Some parts were missing while others had spares,
so wherever she went she drew curious stares.

With all the unusual features she had
you would think that Miss Lulu McDunn would be sad.
But she somehow found good
in the things that were not.
And for someone so small
what was not,
was a lot!

One little bug lived inside Lulu's ear.
When the bug began buzzing
that's all she could hear.
But her heart was quite big
and the bug was quite small,
so to Lulu the bug was no bother at all.

Bzzz

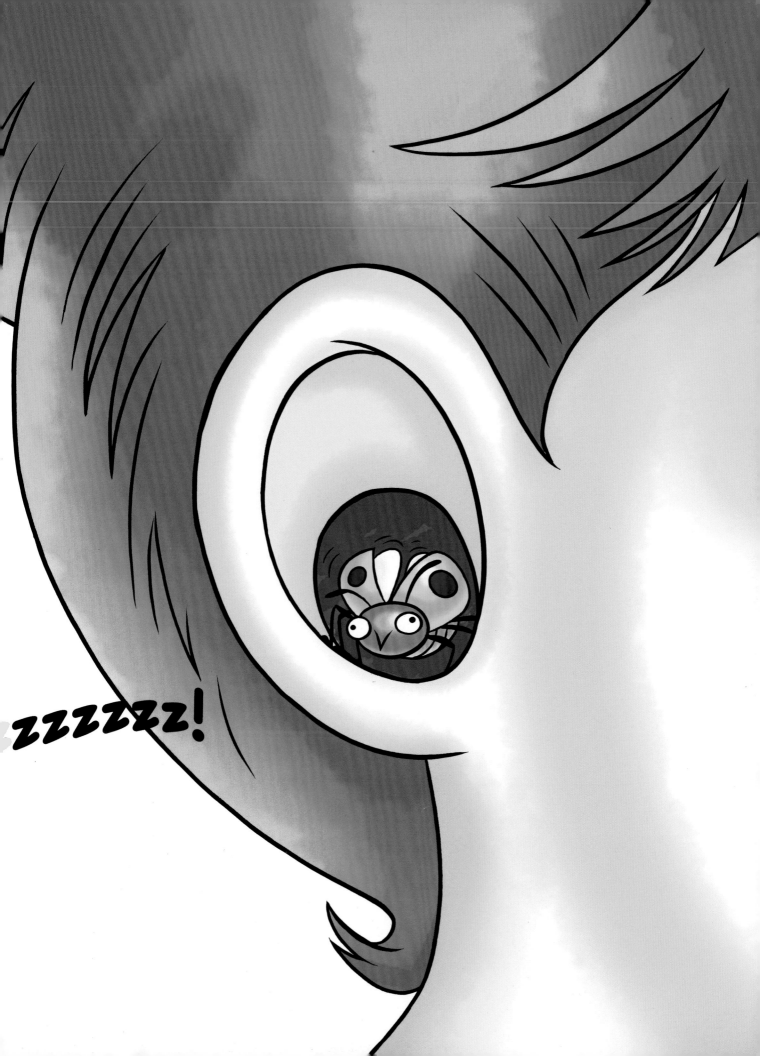

And the buzzing the bug made at night in her head
helped to lull her to sleep as she lay in her bed.
Said Lulu, "The little bug likes living there-
and with two ears I've still got a clear ear to spare."

Bzzzzzzzzzzz!

Two was the number
of eyes in her head.
Her left eye was green
but her right eye was red.
They were spaced far apart
and they weren't quite in line.
But to Lulu the two of her eyes matched up fine.

Said Lulu,
"I see all the good things I've got,
and I choose not to look
at the things I have not.
Having non-matching eyes
doesn't matter to me.
What matters is that
I have two and not three."

Three was the number of birds in her hair.
Her hair was quite high so they nested up there.
It wound all around like the point of a screw.
Its height reached much higher than most hairdos do.

So the birds had to duck
when she passed through a door
or they'd all bump their heads
and wind up on the floor.
Said Lulu, "A nest in my hair keeps it messed.
But as long as they stay, I'll treat each as a guest."

Four was the number of knobs on her knees.
They looked like potatoes but felt like soft cheese.
And she couldn't wear pants 'cause the fit wasn't right.
The thighs fit too loose but the knees fit too tight.

The knobs on her knees
made a squeak when they bent
so you'd always be warned
when she came or she went.
But to Lulu her knee knobs were special
And more-
They padded her knees
when she knelt on the floor.

Squeak!

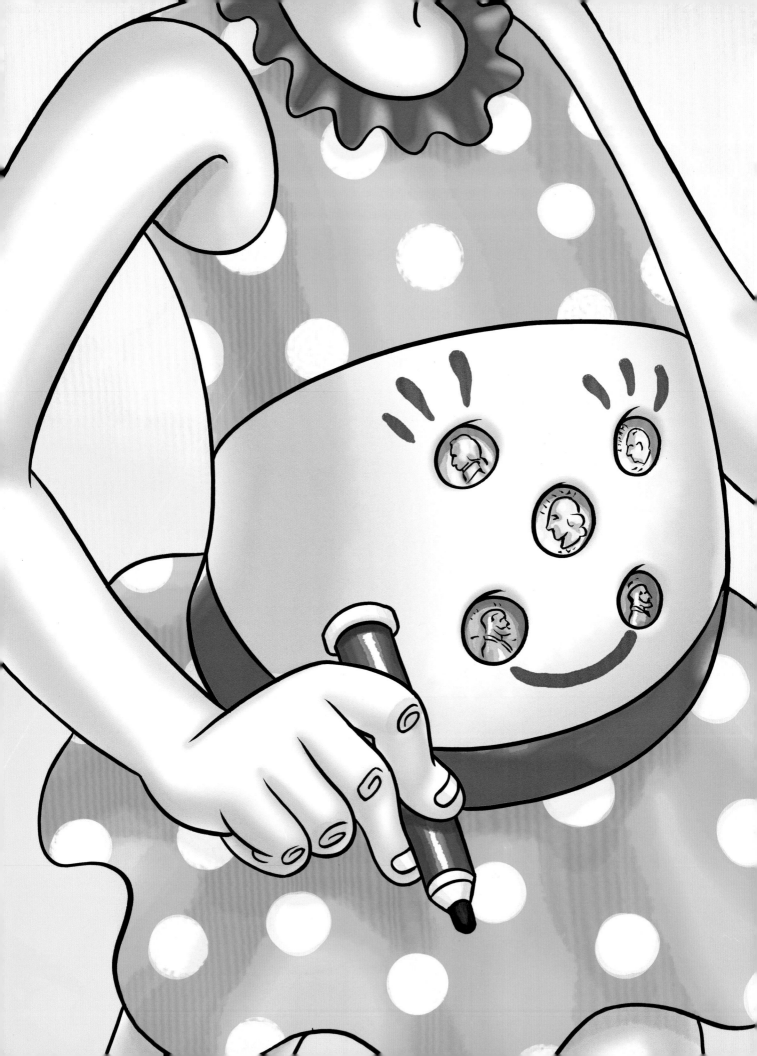

Five buttons she had
where there should have been one.
But Lulu McDunn
thought the buttons were fun.
With a marker she'd make a cute buttonhole face.
And she found that her coins fit each buttonhole space.

She'd hide all her coins when she went to the beach.
With her belly so close they were always in reach.

She wasn't embarrassed
when people would stare.
She was proud of her belly
with buttons to spare.

Six thumbs but no fingers on Lulu's left mitt.
With the size of her hands it's surprising they fit.
They were short.
They were fat.
And they looked like a bunch
of little snack sausages laid out for lunch.

But for opening jars all those thumbs had a grip.
When gripping a jar lid her grip would not slip.
She could twist lids right open
when others could not.
So she liked her six thumbs.
Yes, she liked them a lot.

Seven, the number
of hairs on her nose;
they would curl all around
when humidity rose.
And they swayed back and forth
when a breeze gently blew.
Like streamers they'd flit
from her nose where they grew.

They tickled her cheeks
as they fluttered about.
Lulu liked them so much
she hoped others would sprout.
"You should pull the hairs out."
is what people would say.
But she wouldn't give in; on her
nose they would stay.

Eight was the total of toes that she had.
Just having eight toes would make most people sad.
Four toes on each foot you would think would just stink.
Two toes less than ten is too few you would think.

When she painted
her toenails
she'd finish
too fast.
The fourth toe
she would paint
on each foot
would be last.
Said Lulu,
"Eight toes
are the number
I'd choose,
four toes
on each foot
leave more room
in my shoes."

Nine was the number of teeth in her mouth.
There were four pointing north.
There were five pointing south.
You might think that nine teeth just would not be enough
when chewing on food that was stringy and tough.

Her teeth
were arranged
so whenever
she blew,
sweet music
came out
with the air
that blew through.
She liked
to show off
the few teeth
that she had.
And the tunes
she could blow
through her teeth
made her glad.

Ten was the number
of Miss Lulu's freckles.
But her freckles
were not merely charming
pink speckles.
They looked more like spots
of unusual hue.
The spots were not pink,
but a bright royal blue.

She worried that sunlight
would make the spots fade.
So she always made sure
that she stayed in the shade.
Said Lulu,
"My spots are the only you'll find.
They're a part of what makes me a
one-of-a-kind."

Now some folks might think
that Miss Lulu looked odd
or that some of her parts
didn't fit on her bod.

And she didn't fit in
with the in-fitting crowd,
with their noses so high
and their voices so loud.

Said Lulu, "I'm happy with what I've been blessed.
Each part that I have has its place with the rest.
When the parts are all placed in the place each should be
the sum of the parts all together is *me!*"